More
Bright & Bold
Bulletin Boards

CHRISTINE MENARD

Fort Atkinson, Wisconsin

Many thanks to my husband, Andrew, who spent many hours proofing and editing this book. Thanks also to Andrea, my daughter, who offered helpful suggestions.

Published by Alleyside Press, an imprint of
Highsmith Press LLC
W5527 Highway 106
P.O. Box 800
Fort Atkinson, Wisconsin 53538-0800
1-800-558-2110

© Christine Menard, 1995
Cover design: Frank Neu

The paper used in this publication meets the minimum requirements of American National Standard for Information Science — Permanence of Paper for Printed Library Material. ANSI/NISO Z39.48-1992.

Library of Congress Cataloging-in-Publication Data

Menard, Christine
    More bright & bold bulletin boards / Christine Menard.
       p. cm.
      1. Library exhibits–United States. 2. Bulletin boards-
    -United States. I. Title.
    Z673.5 1995
      021.7–dc20   95-20491
    ISBN 0-917846-61-3

Contents

Introduction

While attractive bulletin boards can be easy and economical to for you to produce, they can improve the whole image of your library, call attention to little used book collections and draw the interest of the infrequent library patron. *More Bright and Bold Bulletin Boards* is full of ideas for specific projects for your library, and to make all of them easier, I have included some timesaving, cost-saving tips picked up along the way. I hope these will be of help to you as you plan your library's bulletin boards.

Cost-saving hints

Some resources and sources for display supplies can be readily found at little expense. Local stores can be approached to donate supplies. Wallpaper stores can be asked to donate old sample books, and the patterned sample pages can be used instead of plain art paper to add interest to the boards. Or have a Christmas/Hanukkah party and ask for art supplies from businesses. Then be sure to send all these local businesses thank you notes.

You can get patrons and staff involved in the search for inexpensive materials too. Ask staff members to save paper bags and gift wrap paper from home. These can also add interest to the board. Write a wanted list for the needed supplies and post it on a bulletin board at your library. Or have a library birthday party and ask for art supplies from patrons. Don't forget to write thank you letters to the donors.

Shop with discounts in mind. In the fabric stores' discount areas, buy solid color fabric remnants to cover display tables. Try looking for baskets and flowers to place near the boards at garage sales.

Be economical. Instead of buying a whole roll of a rarely used art paper like orange or purple, buy only a few feet at a time from a school supply store. Also, replace only the pencil colors that are needed instead of buying an entire box of new colors.

Make your bulletin board area a display area by adding details such as colorful fabrics, book-ends or a basket of flowers. Place a table in front of the board to hold these items and books. Coordinate the accessories to the board's colors, and individualize the details to fit the board's theme.

Making each board unique

Each board can be given a unique look by adding interesting accessories. Use a batik-like cloth to cover the table for "One World, Many Cultures," and add a flat round basket containing seashells. An old-fashioned straw basket with red flowers and a red cloth on the table can improve the appearance of the "Crafty Ideas" board. Dark brown burlap covering the table of the "A Southwestern Direction" board gives it a rugged feel. An artificial cactus in a clay pot could also be added to the table. Real Indian corn can be placed on the table for the "Many Stories to Share" board.

Ask the local ASPCA to donate pamphlets to place near the "Popular Pets" board. Likewise, the local computer club can donate copies of its newsletter to distribute next to the "Compute This! Computers and You!" board. Both the library and the local organization will benefit with this added publicity. Use a printed fabric that looks like an old-fashioned quilt to cover the table for "Long Ago and Far Away." Dried flowers in an old pitcher will also lend a long ago look. Place a bird house next to the "Birds in Our Lives" board, and attach an artificial bird to the house. Borrow whatever your budget can not buy. Your boards will be more attractive with these added details.

Displaying books

Remember to place the books on the table in diverse ways. This makes the board more interesting than placing all the books in black bookends. Some books can stand, others can lay flat or be opened to attractive photos. Use colorful bookends to hold the rest of the books. Use books that are in good condition for your displays.

Continue to look for ideas to individualize the board. Some sources for fresh ideas can come from decorating magazines, books and TV shows on decorating. I make a copy of an interesting idea or write it down. Or, I may cut out ideas from my own magazines. I keep these ideas in a folder labeled "New Ideas."

Timesaving tips

Here are a few timesaving tips that will make bulletin boards quick and easy to produce. Enlarge all patterns at the same time, if possible. And enlarge the pattern on the correct color of paper in pencil. Outline all with a marker at the same time. Please read the directions for each board first, since some items do not need to be outlined. Try to cut all pattern pieces during the same time period.

Use sharp scissors. Clean the blades of the scissors from time to time with soap and water; this removes the glue residues and helps the scissors cut better. Dry thoroughly.

Keep all the art supplies in one place, in order to prevent searching for them each time they are needed. Label empty copier paper boxes to store fabrics, flowers and other display materials. Or keep supplies in clear plastic boxes. Clean all supplies after use. Wipe and cap glues after use.

I have begun to use a glue stick instead of rubber cement for some gluing jobs. Most glue sticks are non-toxic, while most mixtures of rubber cement are toxic. (Check the label to make sure.) Also, when using a glue stick, you can usually peel the picture off, just like with rubber cement. Test several types of glue sticks to find the one that works best for you.

I find that some inexpensive colored pencils can produce results similar to the more expensive ones. Ask to test the ones that you're interested in buying. Colored pencils can be stored in self-closing plastic bags.

Special occasions

I enjoy designing bulletin boards. I find it rewarding to coordinate the bulletin board with special occasions if possible. I try to incorporate illustrations that are related to the board's theme, instead of using ones that are stereotypical. The boards in More Bright & Bold Bulletin Boards might be used to celebrate some of the following:

American History Month
Long Ago & Far Away (February)

Black History Month
African American Firsts (February)

Women's History Month
A Flair for Art... (March)

Craft Month
Crafty Ideas (March)

National Library Week
Read It! (April)

International Children's Book Day
Books for All! (April 2)

Asian Pacific American History Month
Years of the Dragon (May)

Pet Month
Popular Pets (May)

Hispanic Heritage Month
A Southwestern Direction
(September 15-October 15)

Halloween
Mysterious Happenings or Sci-Fi (October)

American Indian Heritage Month
Many Stories to Share (November)

Christmas
Crafty Ideas (December)

We can all learn...

We all can learn by our mistakes. I sure have. Here are some tales of my artistic misadventures. When the "Compute This! Computers and You!" board was first made, oil pastels were used as dots for the backboard. The paper was allowed to dry for a few days since oil pastels smear. But when the board was put up, I still managed to get a few small blotches on my clothes. So now I only use waxy pastels for projects which require little handling.

We designed and made a bird house out of foam core for the "Birds in Our Lives" board that took much too long to put together. It would have been better to have borrowed a wooden one. Our budget didn't allow for real chili peppers for the "A Southwestern Direction" board, so they were made out of a combination of flour and water. This combination took forever to dry in our moist south Louisiana climate and some peppers cracked after drying. They were even placed in a paper closet that had a dehumidifier to keep the paper dry. The peppers should have been made out of poster board.

Storing boards for reuse

Store all bulletin boards for reuse later. Place artwork in commercial or homemade portfolios. Make a portfolio by stapling two poster boards together. You may want to plan to buy a few portfolios or other kinds of storage each year. Place this in your budget. Some artwork can be rolled and placed in empty art paper roll boxes. Print the contents on each portfolio or box. Check on the artwork from time to time to make sure it stays in good condition. Store all artwork away from direct sunlight which could fade it.

Use plastic-coated paper clips to hold together related artwork rather than metal ones, which will rust over time. Remember that artwork glued with rubber cement will come apart after a few years. Be prepared to reglue items if you wish to keep them.

Keep an inventory of all bulletin board artwork. List each bulletin board and the month and year it was displayed to avoid reusing it too soon. You may want to take a color photo of each display and list the items that were used. This information can be placed in a binder where it will be easily found.

Catalogs

You will be able to find many of your art supplies locally at art supply or teacher material stores.

Of course not all art and display supplies are available locally, so you may want to try the catalogs listed below:

Art supplies
Dick Blick
P.O. Box 1267
Galesburg, IL 61402-1267

Colorful bookends and library display items
Highsmith Inc.
W5527 Highway 106
P.O. Box 800
Fort Atkinson, WI 53538-0800

Posters and AV on Women's History
National Women's History Project
7738 Bell Road
Windsor, CA 95492

Each new project, and any problems it created, helped me learn something I could use to design the next board. And I still look forward to the challenge that the designing and producing of each new bulletin board will bring. Make the boards in this handbook your own unique creations by adding to or subtracting from my ideas. Have fun and think creatively!

BIRDS
IN OUR
LIVES

My parents, Rose and Mose St. Julien, take great pleasure in feeding the many birds that visit their small town yard. My creative Dad has rigged up old poles and hubcaps into useful feeders. My Mom always checks to see if there is food for the little birds. I've become a bird watcher in my city yard also. A pair of cardinals daily check the ground for fallen magnolia pods, while several sneaky blackbirds steal the dogs' chow.

Construction

Enlarge the letters on blue art paper using the opaque projector. Cut out the letters. Staple the yellow art paper to the board. Pin and then staple the green border. Pin the letters on the right side of the board.

You and your helper may want to wear gloves to do this part. Cut the garland, using wire cutters, into five large pieces for major branches. Cut eleven smaller pieces for minor branches. Twist minor branches onto major branches. Join the major branches to form a trunk. Try to achieve a natural look. See the illustration. The helper is needed to hold the branches in place while they are being stapled. Staple branches several times in the same area to insure that they will not fall off easily.

Cut a 10" piece of floral wire. Jab one half of the wire through bottom of nest. Stick other end of wire about one inch away. Pull both ends through nest. Twist end of wire securely to attach nest to middle front of branch. Attach one bird to this nest. Attach other birds to various parts of the tree. All birds should have wires for easy mounting. Look at the illustration when placing the birds and nest. Tie a bow on the trunk with the blue ribbon. Use yellow book-ends to hold books.

Supplies

Five 3" artificial birds with attached wires (3 red & 2 blue birds)

small nest

artificial pine garland

thin floral wire

straight pins

wire cutters

cutting board

glue

scissors

bright yellow art paper for background

copier

yellow copier paper for bookmark

stapler

green art paper for border

gloves

blue art craft paper for letters

opaque projector

yellow bookends

1" blue ribbon for bow

Letter Patterns

BIRDS IN OUR LIVES

Bookmark

Use yellow copier paper for the bookmark.

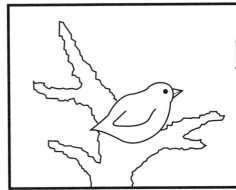

Birds in Our Lives

Bugs sure are neat! Some are graceful, and some are grotesque, but all are so wonderfully complicated for their size. That's what makes the study of their complicated communities and amazing abilities to survive a continuing fascination for old and young alike.

Construction

Cut apart several large paper bags and glue the bags together to make enough paper for the pot. Let dry.

Enlarge the patterns here using the opaque projector: the pot on the glued-together paper bags; the twig on the brown craft paper; one flower and the monarch butterfly on the orange craft paper; the bee's body and a flower on the yellow craft paper; the ladybugs on the red craft paper; the stems, the leaves and the praying mantis on the green craft paper; the letters and a flower on the blue craft paper; the bee's wings on white tissue paper. Draw all in pencil first.

Re-draw the bee, the mantis, the monarch butterfly, and ladybugs using a black marker. Lightly color the mantis with a green colored pencil. Color the monarch butterfly's inner wings with an orange colored pencil. The body and outer edges of the wings should be colored with a black colored pencil. Color the little circles around the edges with a white colored pencil. Use a book on butterflies as a coloring guide.

Cut out all the bugs and wings leaving the black outline. Glue the large wings underneath the bee. Tape black pipe cleaners to the back of the bee's and monarch's heads for antennas.

Outline the flowers, the stems, the leaves, the pot and the twig using a black marker. Also outline the letters. Cut out all of these leaving the black outline. Cut 1"-wide strips of blue craft paper for the border using the cutting board.

Cut light blue craft paper to size and staple it to the board. Pin the letters, the flower pot, the stems, the leaves, the twig and all the bugs as shown in the illustration. Pin the orange flower at the top, then the blue one in the middle and the yellow flower closest to the twig. Staple the border to the board. Use green bookends to hold the majority of the books.

Books

Display books on the many types of insects. Craft and poetry books on bugs can also be included.

Supplies

light blue art craft paper for background	scissors
white tissue paper for wings	stapler
large paper bags for pot	pins
yellow art craft paper for flower and bee	pencil
green copier paper for bookmark	opaque projector
orange art craft paper for flower and butterfly	copier
red art craft paper for ladybugs	green bookends
brown art craft paper for twig	glue
medium blue art craft paper for letters, border, and flower	cutting board
	colored pencils
medium green art craft paper for stems, leaves, and mantis	black medium and large point markers
black pipe cleaners	clear tape

Letter Patterns

BUGS! BUGS! BUGS!

Patterns

Bookmark

Duplicate the bookmark on green copier paper.

Bugs! Bugs! Bugs!

I've always liked baseball—it's a sport I can understand. But I became more interested in the sport when my niece decided to start playing. It's fun to watch her all-girl team play. As my husband Andrew says, "They got a lot of heart."

Construction

Enlarge the letters "Catch a Good Book" in red paper, and the baseball pattern on white art paper, using the opaque projector. Outline the letters and baseball using the black marker, but use the red marker to draw the baseball's stitches. See pattern for placement. Then cut the letters and the baseball out.

Cut the light blue paper to the size of the board. Cover a flat surface with paper to protect it, and place the light blue paper on top. Remove the paper labels from the crayons before using them. Rub a dark brown crayon along the very bottom of the light blue paper to give the impression of stands.

Draw the fans above the stands on the light blue paper with light pencil strokes. Then color the fans with crayons. Draw people with different skin and clothing colors. Look at the patterns for ideas on how to draw the fans. Work on one small area at a time. Draw an oval shape for the face. Add hair next. Hair can be colored red, black, brown, gray, or yellow. It can be short or long, straight or curly. Some people can be bald. Only head, arms, and shirt need to be drawn, since the people are place in the stands. The people need not be drawn in detail or too carefully because they are supposed to be far away.

Using the cutting board, cut 1"-wide strips of black craft paper for the border. Staple light blue craft paper to the board for the background. Staple the border to the board. Pin baseball to left top section of the board. Pin letters at an angle to the right of the ball. Draw action marks around ball and letters with the black color. Use red book-ends to hold the majority of the books.

Books

Display fiction and non-fiction books on baseball and other sports.

Supplies

black art craft paper for border	cutting board
light blue art craft paper for background	scissors
white art craft paper for baseball	stapler
red art craft paper for letters	pins
crayon colors	opaque projector
black medium point marker	copier
red medium point marker	red bookends
red copier paper for bookmarks	pencil

Letter Patterns

CATCH A
GOOD BOOK!

Patterns

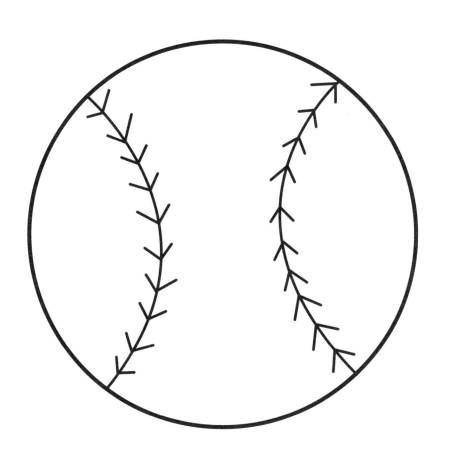

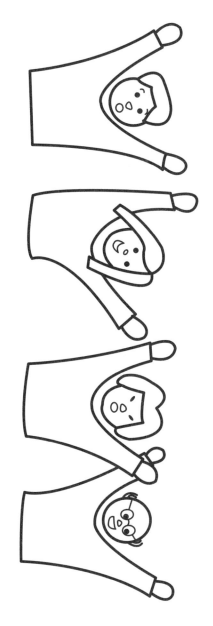

Bookmark

Duplicate the bookmark on red copier paper.

 Catch a Good Book!

Books on Sports

I like computers because they can retain information and copy and paste. So retyping an entire page for one mistake is a thing of the past. Since I hunt and peck and spell with lots of imagination, computers are great in my book.

Construction

Use the opaque projector to enlarge the computer screen on white art paper; the computer, the mouse, and the plug on gray paper or poster board; the letters on black art paper; and the curved letter strips on red art paper. Outline all the pieces in pencil. Draw the smiley face on the white screen in pencil. Then redraw all the pieces in black marker except the letters, and cut out. Glue the screen to the computer. Arrange and glue the letters to the curved strip.

With the cutting board, cut 1"-wide strips of red craft paper for the border. Cut the white paper to the size of the board. Cover a flat surface with paper to protect it from the markers, and place the white paper on top. Use the red, blue and green markers to dot the white paper, giving the illusion of a large computer screen. Let dry.

Pin and then staple the dotted paper to the board. Pin the letter strips, the computer, the mouse and the plug as shown in the illustration. Cut the black yarn to curve and fit the area between the computer and the mouse, and the computer and the plug. Tape the yarn to the back of the computer, plug and mouse. Then pin the yarn in a curve. Staple the border to the board. Use red bookends to hold the majority of the books.

Books

Display books about computers.

Supplies

red art craft paper for border and letter strips

white art craft paper for background

gray paper or poster board for computer

black art craft paper for letters

white copier paper for bookmark

black, blue, red, and green markers

black yarn

clear tape

cutting board

scissors

stapler

pins

pencil

glue

copier

opaque projector

red bookends

Bookmark

Duplicate the bookmark on white paper.

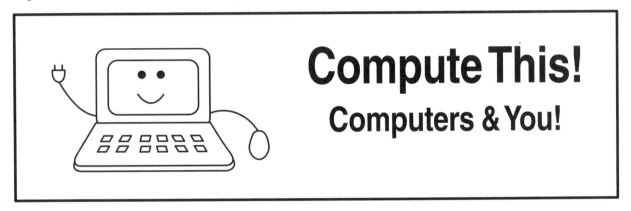

PATTERNS

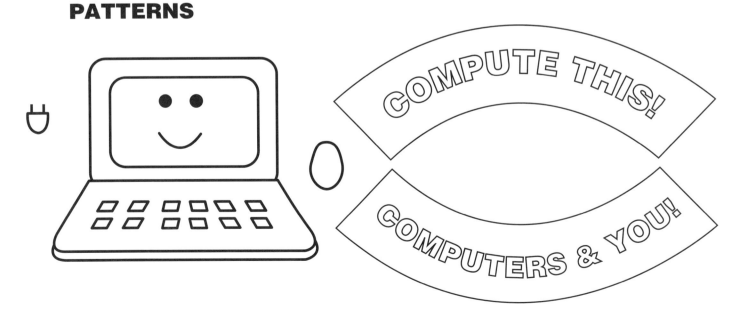

A lot of my small cash goes into purchasing craft and art supplies. Finding a craft book with new craft ideas is exciting. My philosophy is that everyone and anyone can do crafts. They're fun and relaxing, and I think finishing a project successfully can also build up a person's self-esteem.

Construction

Enlarge all the pattern pieces in pencil using the opaque projector: the rectangle, the duck's eye and curved shape on yellow paper; the duck and its wing on white paper; the duck's bill, the paintbrush holder, and the pencil on orange paper; the letters and the bow on red paper; the pencil point on tan paper; the ruler on blue paper; the paintbrush tip on black; and the paintbrush stick on green.

Use the black marker to outline the pieces, and then cut all of them out. Arrange and glue the letters to the curved strip. Glue the brush holder to the paintbrush stick, the brush to the holder, and the pencil point to the pencil. Glue the bill, the eye, and the bow to the duck. Place and glue the pencil, ruler, and paintbrush under the wing as shown in the illustration.

Cut 1"-wide strips of red craft paper with the cutting board for the border. Braid the red yarn into two pieces, which are used to "hang" the yellow rectangle.

Staple blue paper to the board for the background. Pin the yellow rectangle, the curved shape and the duck as shown in the illustration. Hide the yarns' ends and pin the braided yarn between the curved shape and the rectangle. Staple the border to the board. Use yellow bookends to hold majority of the books.

Books

Display books on all kinds of crafts.

Supplies

medium blue art craft paper for background

yellow art craft paper for sign shapes

red art craft paper for letters, border, and bow

black medium point marker

green, white, orange, tan, and black art craft
    paper for pencil, ruler, paint brush, and
    duck

yellow copier paper for bookmark

cutting board

scissors

yellow bookends

pins

opaque projector

copier

stapler

pencil

glue

red yarn for sign

Bookmark

Duplicate the bookmark on yellow paper.

19

Patterns

Libraries are *great!* Not only do libraries loan CD's, video tapes, and audio books but many also loan toys and computer games. Where else can you take something home to use for free? Many people are amazed when they find out all the things a library offers. So amaze your patrons and point out all the non-book items your library offers.

Construction

Of course you will want to reproduce only the AV materials that your library owns. Reproduce several copies of the same item, if need be, to fill up the space.

Enlarge these patterns using the opaque projector: record and letters on black craft paper; CD's center part, record's center part, video case, and bag's details, and handle on medium blue craft paper; computer and CD circle on light gray craft paper; magazine, phone, and cassette case on red craft paper; newspaper on cream paper; bag, computer screen, cassette and video reels on white paper. Draw all in pencil first. Then redraw all, except the letters and the record, using a black marker.

Cut out all the parts leaving the black outline. Glue CD's blue center part to the gray CD. The record's blue center part needs to be glued to the large black record. Glue the bag's blue details and handle onto the white bag. The white computer screen needs to be glued onto the gray computer. Cut out the inside oval of the red cassette case and the two rectangles on the blue video case. Glue the red cassette case on top of the cassette's white reel set, and the blue video case on top of the video's white reel part. Make sure the reels are centered for both. Let all dry.

Lightly color around the gray part of the CD with blue and red pencil colors to recreate a shine.

Cut 1"-wide strips of medium blue craft paper with the cutting board for the border. Cut yellow craft paper to size and staple it to the board. Pin the letters and all the AV materials as shown in the illustration. Tape one end of a piece of red yarn under the phone, and the other end to the phone handle. Pin the yarn as needed. Staple the border to the board. Use yellow bookends to hold the majority of the books.

Books

Display AV materials for check-out and library use.

Supplies

black art craft paper for record and letters

white copier paper for bookmark

yellow art craft paper for background

medium blue art craft paper for border, CD, bag, record, and video

light gray art craft paper for computer and CD

red art craft paper for magazine, phone, and cassette

cream paper for newspaper

white art craft paper for computer, bag, cassette, and video

scissors

stapler

pins

pencil

opaque projector

copier

yellow bookends

black markers

colored pencils

glue

red yarn for phone

clear tape

Letter Patterns

DON'T JUST BOOK IT !

Patterns

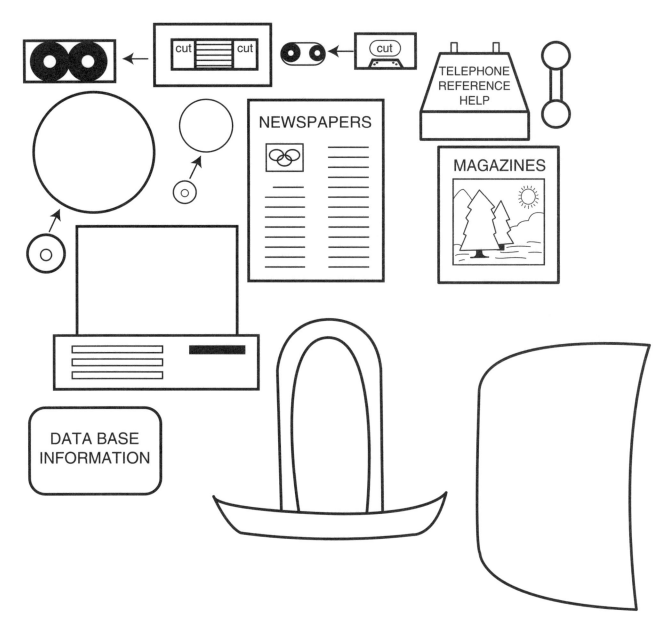

Bookmark

Duplicate the bookmark on white copier paper.

Who doesn't love weird things? It's hard to resist sneaking a peek at the latest tabloid's bold headlines declaring that UFOs were sighted in Florida, or that Elvis and Marilyn Monroe were seen boarding the subway in New York. Since I also love to read about strange occurrences I decided to make this board.

Construction

Glue the aluminum foil onto the white art paper. Allow to dry for about half an hour. Use the green and black markers to make random streaks across the foil. Allow to dry.

Using the opaque projector, enlarge the letters "Mysterious Happenings" on the foil side. Use a pencil to draw the letters, and then outline them in black marker. Also enlarge the silhouettes of Bigfoot, Nessie and three UFOs in pencil on black paper. Then cut out the letters and the silhouettes.

Cut the dark blue paper to the size of the board and staple it to the board for the background. Pin letters and the silhouettes of Bigfoot, Nessie and the UFOs as shown in the illustration. Then adjust these and staple them. Tear or cut netting into uneven strips. Pin the strips across the board and over the letters, making sure the netting doesn't completely cover the letters. Anchor the white artificial cobwebs onto the pins holding the netting. Place the cobwebs sparingly to produce a natural effect. Use the black bookends to hold the majority of the books.

Books

Display fiction and nonfiction books on mysterious occurrences such as UFOs, ghosts, Bigfoot, Nessie and strange disappearances.

Supplies

dark blue art craft paper for background

black netting for background

white art craft paper for letters

black art craft paper for silhouettes

aluminum foil for letters

black permanent marker

white artificial cobwebs (available during
    Halloween)

white copier paper for bookmark

pins

opaque projector

glue stick

black bookends

pencil

copier

scissors

stapler

Letter Patterns

MYSTERIOUS HAPPENINGS

Bookmark

Duplicate the bookmark on white copier paper.

Patterns

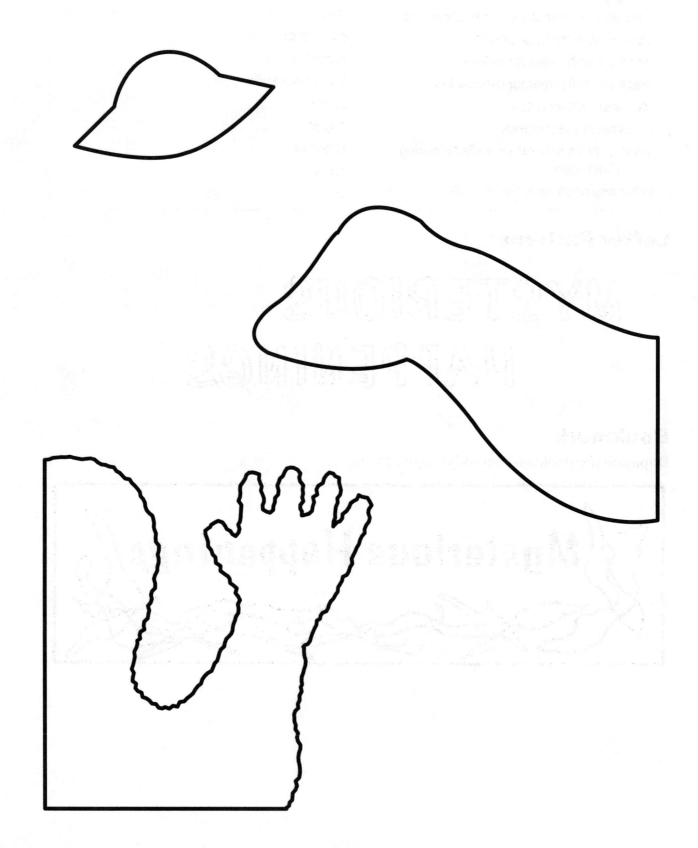

POPULAR PETS

Five good reasons why I decided to design a board on pets include our pet-loving daughter Andrea and our family pets. All are unique, but Alix, a long and lean part-Siamese feline who relishes galloping through our house and dancing on freshly dried towels is definitely the weirdest. Then there are our two female mutts; Sandy who is cute and sweet, and old Red who still loves a good dog fight. Lastly there's Sweety, a feisty little blue parakeet who constantly jousts with his swing to the undivided attention and amusement of Alix.

Construction

Enlarge these patterns using the opaque projector: the mouse on the paper bag; the rabbit on the white craft paper; the snake on the light green craft paper; the parrot's eye on the light pink craft paper; the parrot's head on the red craft paper; the parrot's shoulder and the lizard on the medium green craft paper; the parrot's tail, and the letters on the medium blue craft paper; the cat on the light gray craft paper; the "floor," the pole, and parrot's perch on the medium brown craft paper. Draw all in pencil first.

Redraw the mouse, the cat, the lizard, the snake and the rabbit using a black marker. Color the pets using colored pencils. Use browns and grays for the mouse's head and pink for its paws and nose. Color the cat's eyes with yellow. Lightly color the snake and the lizard with greens and yellows. Cut out all the pets leaving the black outline. Glue the mouse in the crook of the cat's tail.

Also redraw the parrot using a black marker. Color the parrot using colored pencils. Use black to fill in the parrot's beak as shown in the illustration. Color the red head part with red and around the ends of these feathers with bright green. The green

27

shoulder part can be colored with green and the edges of these feathers should be colored with blue. The parrot's tail part can be colored with blue. Coloring the ends of the feathers in each section the color of the next part helps the parts blend together. Refer to books on parrots if more coloring information is needed. Cut out the parrot leaving the black outline. Match the dotted lines when gluing the parrot. Glue the red parrot's head section on top of the pink eye section, then the head on top of the green shoulder. Glue the shoulder on top of the blue tail section to complete the bird. Let dry.

Outline the "floor", the pole, and the parrot's perch using a black marker. Also outline the letters. Cut out all these leaving the black outline.

Cut 1"-wide strips of medium blue craft paper with the cutting board for the border.

Cut yellow craft paper to size and staple it to the board. Pin the letters, the "floor", the pole, and parrot's perch and all the pets as shown in the illustration. Staple the border to the board. Use blue bookends to hold the majority of the books.

Books

Display fiction and nonfiction books on the all kinds of pets.

Supplies

yellow art craft paper for background	scissors
light pink art craft paper for parrot	stapler
paper bag for mouse	pins
medium gray art craft paper for cat	pencil
yellow copier paper for bookmark	opaque projector
light green art craft paper for snake	copier
red art craft paper for parrot	blue bookends
white art craft paper for rabbit	pencil colors
medium blue art craft paper for parrot, letters, and border	cutting board
	glue
medium green art craft paper for parrot and lizard	black medium and large point markers
medium brown art craft paper for "floor," pole, and parrot's perch	

Letter Patterns

POPULAR PETS

Patterns

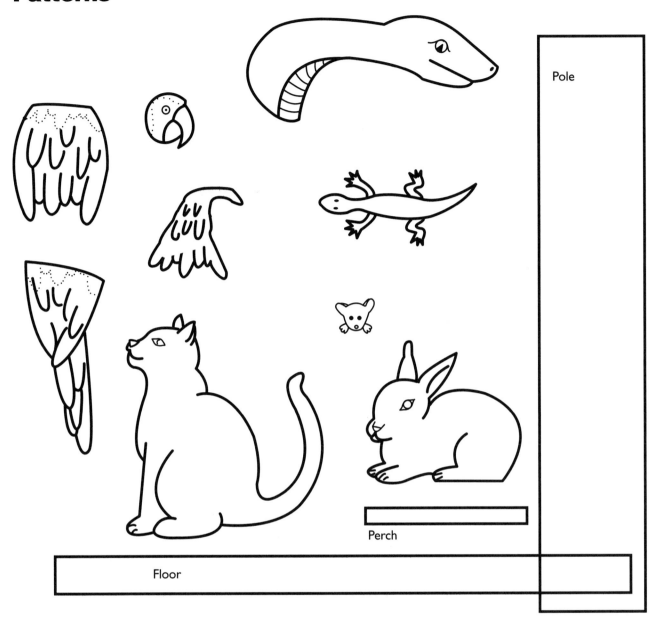

Pole

Perch

Floor

Bookmark

Duplicate the bookmark on yellow copier paper.

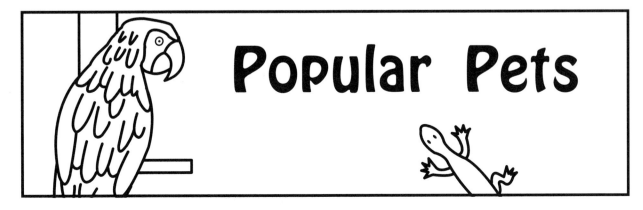

Popular Pets

Flags are more than just cloth; they are a symbol of the people who live in a country. Some flag designs are hundreds of years old, while others are just as new as the emerging nations they represent. I decided to incorporate this interest in the beauty and history of flags to liven up this board's design.

Construction

Use the opaque projector to enlarge the words "Books for All!" and "International Children's Book Day" on black craft paper, the book on red craft paper, and pages on white craft paper. Also enlarge all the children's faces and hands on white craft paper, their hair on black craft paper, and their bodies, one each on medium blue, yellow, and green. The flags should be in these colors: France–⅓ medium blue, ⅓ white, and ⅓ red; Vietnam: red field and yellow star; Gabon –⅓ medium blue, ⅓ yellow, and⅓ green;

Japan– white field and red circle; and Mali– ⅓ green, ⅓yellow, and ⅓red. Draw all in pencil first.

Cut out the letters, the red book, and the white pages. Glue the red book on top of the white pages. Allow the pages to peek over the top of the book. Draw light pencil lines on the front of the book to use as a guide for gluing the letters. Place and arrange the letters before gluing.

Outline the hands, the body and draw all the parts of the faces with the black marker. Color one face and hand pinkish tan, color another face and hand tannish brown, and the last face should be colored yellowish tan. Cut out the children's faces, hands, hair and bodies. Glue the black braids on the pink-tan face and then glue the face to the medium blue body. Glue the curly hairdo to the brown-tan face and then glue the face onto the yellow body. Then glue the last hair piece to the yellowish tan face and glue that face on the green body.

Cut out all parts of the flags and paper clip each flag part together. Glue the flags in this manner: France– medium blue, white and then red; Vietnam– the yellow star on the red field; Gabon– medium blue, yellow and then green; Japan– the red circle centered on the white field; and Mali– green, yellow and then red.

Cut a piece of light blue craft paper the size of the board and then staple it to the board. Pin the book to the bottom of the board, and pin the children as shown in the illustration. Drape and pin a piece of black yarn across the top of the board for hanging the flags. Hang the flags in this order from left to right: France with medium blue at the top; Vietnam; Gabon with medium blue at top; Japan; and Mali with green at the top. Cut 1"-wide strips of black craft paper with the cutting board and then staple them to the board for the border. Staple parts as needed. Place red bookends to hold the books.

Books

Display books on children of different cultures as well as books in different languages.

Supplies

- light blue craft paper for background
- black craft paper for letters, border, and hair
- white craft paper for flags, faces, pages, and hands
- red craft paper for book and flags
- medium blue craft paper for flags and clothes
- yellow and green craft paper for flags and bodies
- red copier paper for bookmark
- red bookends
- ruler
- scissors
- stapler
- pins
- opaque projector
- pencil
- black medium point marker
- cutting board
- colored pencils
- copier
- glue stick
- black yarn to hang flags

Letters Patterns

BOOKS FOR ALL!
International Children's Book Day

Patterns

Bookmark

Duplicate bookmark on red paper.

Books for All!

International Children's Book Day

Fantasy

The graceful unicorn has been revered for centuries. It was said to have spiritual and magical powers. No wonder it has been connected to books on fantasy. I enjoy fantasy and especially like the imaginative artwork on most fantasy book covers.

Construction

Use the opaque projector to enlarge the letters "Fantasy" on black craft paper and the unicorn oval on white drawing paper. Cut out the letters, but not the unicorn oval until after it is colored.

Outline the unicorn and the oval shape with a black marker. Lightly shade the unicorn's face and mane with light purple.

Shade inside the double oval lines, alternately coloring areas light purple, light pink, and light mint green. Make several bands of these color combinations.

Cut a piece of purple craft paper the size of the board and then staple it to the board. Cut 1"-wide strips of black craft paper with the cutting board and staple to the board for the border. Pin the unicorn to the top left of board. Pin letters to the bottom right of unicorn. Place black bookends to hold the books.

Books

Display books on fantasy by juvenile and adult authors.

Supplies

purple craft paper for background

black craft paper for letters and border

white drawing paper for unicorn /oval

black medium point marker

pencil colors

opaque projector

cutting board

black bookends

copier

light purple copier paper for bookmark

scissors

stapler

pins

pencil

Letter Patterns

Pattern

Bookmark

Duplicate bookmark on light purple copier paper.

Long Ago &
Far Away!

VOTES FOR WOMEN

I've always been interested in long ago times. Since my family has lived in the same area for generations, many old photos of our ancestors have survived. My father used to tell us stories about Nonque Belane (Uncle Belane) and Grand Mere St. Julien (Grandmother St. Julien). I looked forward to those stories, and have very fond memories of those times.

Construction

Use the opaque projector to enlarge the letters, the illustration and the flag stripes (three long and three short stripes) on white craft paper. Also enlarge the small flag section in blue craft paper and the large flag piece in red paper. Draw all in pencil first. Outline all the pieces using a black marker. Make the lines around the edge of the illustration thicker. Erase any pencil lines that show.

Color the illustration with colored pencils. First color the suffragette's hair reddish brown, the face and hand pinkish tan, the hat yellow. the dress and the hat flowers medium blue. Leave the sign and the lace on the collar and sleeve white. Next color the Black sax player's hair and bow tie black, the face and hand brownish tan, the sax yellow, the suit dark blue. Leave the shirt white. Then, color the pioneer woman's hair dark brown, the face and hands tan, the shawl red, the dress dark blue, the gun stock brown and the gun barrel gray. Leave the bonnet and the apron white. Color the Native American's hair black, the face and hand dark tan, and the blanket stripes red, green and blue. Color the basket yellow and the corn brown and red. Draw many small ovals on the corn cobs with the black marker to resemble kernels. Color the two pine trees green. Lastly, color the area below the pines and the corn basket a greenish brown. Cut out this illustration.

Make the flag. Cut out the white stripes, and the red and blue flag sections. Glue the white stripes on the red paper. Draw horizontal pencil lines lightly across the blue section to align the letters. Adjust, then glue the white letters on the blue section. Finally, glue the blue flag section on the left of the red and white striped paper. Cut a piece of white craft paper the size of the board. Pin this white paper to the board and then staple it. Cut 1"-wide strips of dark blue craft paper, with the cutting board, for the border.

Pin the border to the board. Place and pin the flag on the top left and the illustration on the top right. Adjust all so that the bottom of the pioneer woman's dress touches the border, and the flag is behind the suffragette and the Black man. Staple all to the board. Place red bookends to hold the books.

Books

Display books on historical fiction.

Supplies

dark blue craft paper for flag and border	pins
white craft paper for background, letters, illustration and flag	pencil / eraser
	opaque projector
black permanent marker	cutting board
red copier paper for bookmark	colored pencils
red craft paper for flag	copier
scissors	glue stick
stapler	red bookends

Letters Patterns

Patterns

Flag parts

Bookmark

Duplicate the bookmark on blue copier paper.

Long Ago & Far Away!

Historical Fiction

READ IT!

National Library Week

What's fun and exciting and enlightening and inspiring and relaxing and… Yep it's a good book. One of those you can't put down but don't want to finish because it's *sooo* good. One of those you really want the author to write a sequel on. So celebrate reading with this rainbow-colored board and write a fan letter to your favorite author.

Construction

Using the opaque projector, enlarge the letters, the silhouettes of items that represent different genres, and the book jacket on black art paper, while enlarging the book pages on white art paper. Draw them in pencil. Then cut everything out.

Draw lines across the pages lightly in pencil. Glue the white pages onto the black cover. Print genres of books such as historical fiction, westerns, fantasy, mysteries, science fiction and romance in pencil; then, rewrite them in black marker.

Cut 1" strips of black paper for the border. Measure the width and the length of the bulletin board to cut the colorful strips for the background. Divide the width into five sections, and when cutting each section add an inch to each color for overlap, except the strip of red, which should be cut two inches wider than the other strips.

Pin the strips in this order from left to right: red, orange, yellow, green and blue to the bulletin board. Overlap each strip of the background one inch. Pin and adjust the background as needed. Staple it after it is correct. Arrange and pin the book as shown in the illustration. Pin up the letters and the silhouettes above the book and the border sections around edge of board. Staple items to board if needed.

Book Subjects

Place award winning books near this board.

Supplies

art craft paper: red, orange, yellow, green, blue, white, and black

black marker

ruler

copier

yellow bookends

yellow copier paper for bookmarks

pins

pencil

scissors

glue stick

opaque projector

stapler

cutting board

Letter Patterns

READ IT!
National Library Week

Patterns

Bookmark

Duplicate the bookmark on yellow copier paper.

Dreams of the Future

Many people follow science fiction to get a glimpse of what the future may hold. I remember the premiere showing of the first *Star Trek* movie in our city. The movie attracted large crowds. Everyone was excited. Science fiction and fact have seem to merge in our fast paced world.

Construction

Using the opaque projector enlarge the small planets and the letter strips in yellow paper, the city and the large planet on light blue paper, the letters in black paper, and the bubble and the spaceship in white paper. Draw all in pencil first. Then use the black marker to outline the planets, the city, the bubble and the spaceship.

Color some pieces with pencil colors. Color the spaceship's body gray and the circle and semicircle yellow. Color the large planet's rings blueish-purple and the sphere with patches of yellow, purple and light blue. Look at color illustrations of planets. Color the small circles and rectangles of the city yellow and rub blues and purples on the buildings. Then cut out all these pieces and also the letters and letter strips.

Cut the black paper to the exact size of the board for the background. Then cut the dark blue paper to fit the lower fourth of the board below the bubble. Lay the blue paper and the bubble on the black paper and lightly mark where they will be placed on the black paper. Remove them and then use an old toothbrush to splatter white paint on the other areas of the black paper. These splatters will represent distant stars. Test on scrap paper before attempting the large piece of black paper. Apply a small amount of paint to the bristles. Hold the brush in one hand and rub your thumb over the brush to spatter the paint over the paper. Repeat this until the black paper is covered. Let dry for about an hour.

Cut 1"-wide strips of black craft paper with the cutting board for a border for the bottom of the board. Staple the paint-splattered black paper to the board. Pin the blue background paper to the bottom part of the board. Then pin the bubble, the city, the letter strips, the letters the spaceship and the planets on the board as shown in the illustration. Adjust and then, staple all to the board. Staple the black border to blue bottom of the board. Use blue bookends to hold the majority of the books.

Books

Display science fiction books near this display

Supplies

light blue craft paper for city and large planet

dark blue craft paper for background bottom

white craft paper for bubble and space ship

yellow craft paper for letter strips and small planets

black large point marker

black craft paper for border, letters and background

blue bookends

light blue copier paper for bookmarks

pins

pencil / eraser

scissors

opaque projector

stapler

cutting board

colored pencils

white acrylic paint

old toothbrush

Letter Patterns

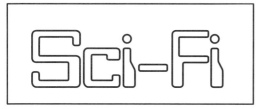

Patterns

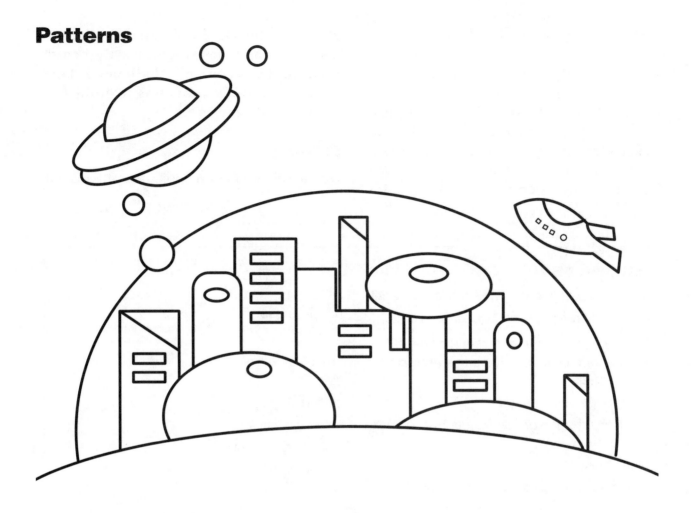

Bookmark

Duplicate bookmark on light blue copier paper.

WISE WORDS

Famous Poems

One of the poems that I love is *Sea Fever* by John Masefield. Since it was my favorite childhood poem, I memorized it for a high school speech class. I've always enjoyed poetry and have even written a few simple poems. Christina Rossetti, Langston Hughes, Nikki Giovanni, and Shel Silverstein are some of my favorite poets. I think that everybody loves some form of poetry, so I decided to design a bulletin board that would focus attention on it.

Construction

Use the opaque projector to enlarge the letters "Wise Words" and the feather on red paper; the ink bottle label and the scroll on white or cream paper and the ink bottle on black paper. Draw all the pieces in pencil.

Cut the light blue paper to the exact size of the board. Then use the opaque projector to enlarge the curving lines on the light blue paper using a pencil. Cover a flat surface with extra paper to protect it and place the light blue paper on top. Redraw the lines using the medium point black marker. Erase all pencil marks that show. Let the blue paper dry flat for about ten minutes.

Use the same flat surface covered with extra paper to layout the other pieces for outlining. Outline all the pieces except the ink bottle using a large black marker. Use the medium point black marker to draw the lines inside of the feather. Print the words "Famous Poems" on the scroll and print "ink" on the label in pencil. Then use a ruler to draw horizontal lines on the scroll in pencil. Print the names of several poets and the titles of their poems on the horizontal lines in pencil. Choose poets and poems that are appropriate for your patrons. Then reprint the words using the medium point black marker. Let each piece dry flat for about ten minutes.

Erase all the pencil marks that show. Cut out all the pieces.

Pin and then staple the blue paper to the bulletin board. Cut 1"-wide strips of black craft paper with the cutting board. Staple the black strips to the bulletin board for the border. Pin letters, the feather, the ink bottle and the scroll to the board. Arrange them as shown in the illustration and then staple them. Place red bookends to hold the books.

Books

Display poetry books, books on poets, and those that show how to write poetry.

Supplies

red craft paper for letters and feather

light blue craft paper for background

black craft paper for border and ink

red copier paper for bookmark

black medium and large point markers

white or cream craft paper for scroll and label

cutting board

opaque projector

ruler

scissors

stapler

pins

pencil / eraser

glue stick

red bookends

Letter Patterns

WISE WORDS

PATTERNS

feather will go here

Bookmark

Duplicate bookmark on red paper.

Wise Words...
Famous Poems

A FLAIR FOR ART

AMERICAN WOMEN ARTISTS

Art has always been one of my favorite subjects. I've always enjoyed painting and drawing and reading about great artists. Until recently, there have been few women artists mentioned in the art books. Thankfully, now there are more books on women artists, and this board is dedicated to them.

Construction

Enlarge the faces of the artists faces including the paint outline surrounding each on the copier to the proper size. Then copy them on the following colored sheets: red, Cassatt; orange, Martinez; yellow, Ringgold; green, Wong; blue, Hunter; and purple, O'Keefe. Cut them out.

Enlarge the sign, "March is Women's History Month" on hot pink copier paper.

Enlarge the letters "A Flair for Art... American Women Artists" in black paper using the opaque projector. Use the opaque projector to enlarge the palette on brown paper, the paint brush stick on black, the holder on a scrap of yellow copier paper and the bristles on black paper.

Cut out the letters, palette and paint brush. Glue the bristles to the holder and the holder to the stick. Cut 1"-wide strips of black craft paper with the cutting board for the border.

Cut the hot pink paper to the size of the board and staple. Also staple the strips of black craft paper to the board for the border. Pin palette to the center of the board. Pin the paint spots and artist's faces as shown in the illustration, starting from the top left: Cassatt; Martinez; Ringgold; Wong; Hunter; and O'Keefe. Pin the paint brush and letters as shown in the illustration. If this display is used in March, place the sign "March is Women's History Month" on a bookend near the board. Black bookends can be used to hold the books.

Books

Place books on women artists and art techniques on display.

Supplies

hot pink paper for background

brown craft paper for palette

bright yellow, green, blue, purple, red, orange, and white copier paper for paint spots

hot pink copier paper for bookmark and sign

black craft paper for border, letters and paint brush

opaque projector

scissors

stapler

pins

copier with enlargement feature

black bookends

cutting board

Letter Patterns

A FLAIR FOR ART...
AMERICAN WOMEN ARTISTS

Bookmark

Duplicate bookmark on hot pink paper.

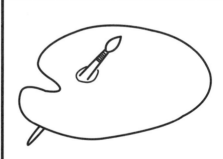

A Flair for Art...
American Women Artists

March

is

Women's History Month

Patterns

Mary Cassatt
Impressionist Painter
(1844–1926)

Maria Martinez
Potter of Pueblo Ceramics
(1881–1980)

Faith Ringgold
Fabric Artist
(1930–   )

Jade Snow Wong
Potter of Chinese Ceramics
(1922–   )

Patterns

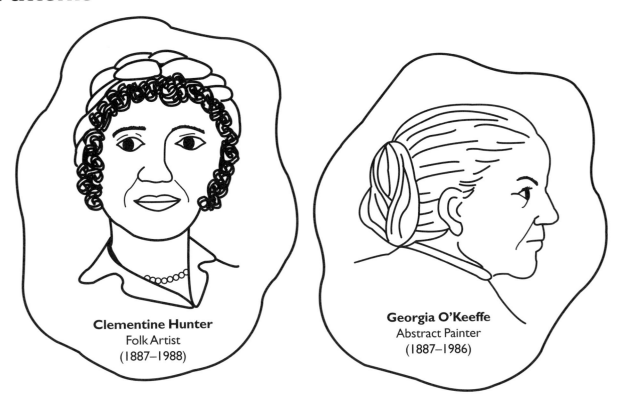

Clementine Hunter
Folk Artist
(1887–1988)

Georgia O'Keeffe
Abstract Painter
(1887–1986)

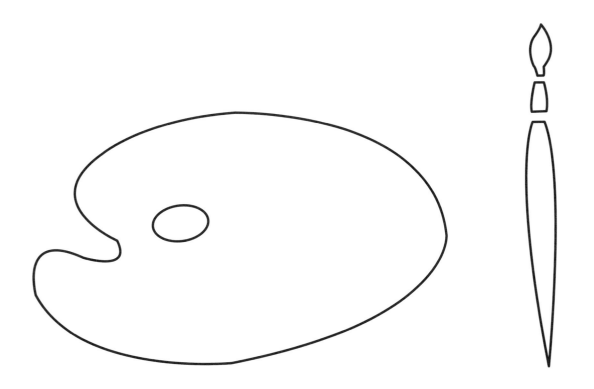

A SOUTHWESTERN DIRECTION

The southwest is a unique area. I had the opportunity to ride on a train through Texas, Arizona, New Mexico and southern California. Most of this section of the U.S. is starkly beautiful. Rocks, rocks, and more rocks on a cascade of barren mountains. It was quite a difference from our lush green southern Louisiana.

Construction

Use the opaque projector to enlarge the letters on red paper and the picture on the poster using pencil. Then outline all the lines on the poster in black marker. Make the border lines thicker than the rest of the picture. Cut out the letters.

Paint the picture using acrylic paints. Wash the brushes after using each color. Use the ¾" brush for large areas, the ½" brush for medium areas, and the ¼" brush for small areas. Allow each color to dry before painting another area.

Alternate red and mustard yellow for the border triangles. Paint the corners bright blue and green. Paint the sky bright blue. Add a bit of white to the brown to paint the jagged cliffs, and use the regular brown to paint the foreground. Paint the moon with mustard yellow, and the cactus with dark green paint. Paint the coyote white. Leave coyote's muzzle, inside of ear, and throat white. Mix white with brown to get a tan color. Paint the tan color over the wet white paint to get a streaked coyote coat. Allow all to dry. Trim poster if needed.

Cut about 25 chile peppers out of the double-sided red poster. Color the stem part with a green pencil color on both sides. Cut a very small slit into both sides of the chili stem. Twist the string around the stems several times so that it is inserted into the slits. Arrange the chiles so that they will hang in a bunch.

Cut 1"-wide strips of brown craft paper with the cutting board for the border. Use the black marker to make wood grain lines on the brown paper. Staple the blue paper to board for the background. Pin the burlap, the peppers, the picture and the letters as shown in the illustration. Staple the border to the board. Use red bookends to hold the majority of the books. If this display is used in September or October, enlarge the sign "Celebrate Hispanic Heritage Month!" on red copier paper, and place it on a bookend near the display.

Books

Display fiction and nonfiction books on the southwest area including crafts, food and celebrations.

Supplies

blue craft paper for background
red craft paper for letters
brown craft paper for border
1/4", 1/2", and 3/4"- wide paint brushes
double-sided red poster for peppers
dark green, white, dark red, brown, mustard yellow, and bright blue acrylic paint for picture
green pencil color
red copier paper for bookmark and sign
white poster board for picture

black permanent marker
copier with enlargement feature
opaque projector
scissors
red bookends
pins
stapler
tan burlap fabric
string to hang peppers
pencil

Letter Patterns

Sign

Celebrate
Hispanic Heritage Month!

Patterns

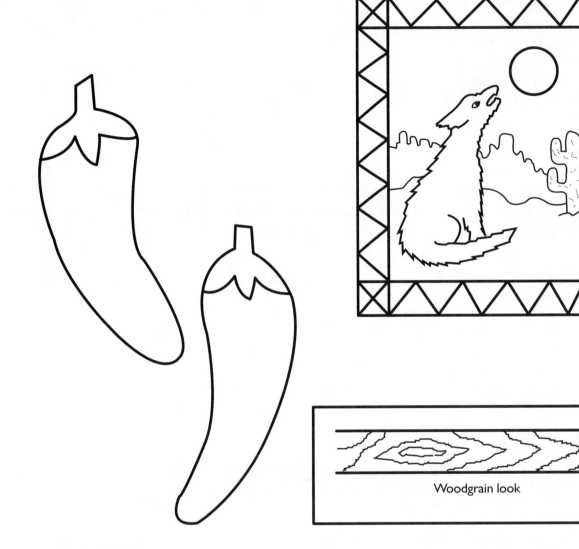

Woodgrain look

Bookmark

Duplicate bookmark on red paper.

A SOUTHWESTERN DIRECTION

AFRICAN AMERICAN FIRSTS

1ST

Isn't it interesting to find out when something was done for the first time? This board highlights several notable "first" achievements of African Americans. It's perfect to use during Black History Month and can be adapted to celebrate important firsts during other special ethnic or historical celebrations. Students can be encouraged to discover more African American firsts to add to the "star questions" already on the board.

Construction

Enlarge all the pattern pieces in pencil using the opaque projector: the letters on black paper; the ten stars on yellow paper; and the 1st on red paper. Outline the stars and the 1st with a large-point marker.

Cut out the ten yellow stars. Lightly draw pencil lines across five of the stars for the questions. Print one question on each star in pencil. Lightly draw pencil lines across each of the last five stars. Use the pencil to print one answer on each of these stars. Then trace over all the pencil printing with the medium point marker. Cut out the letters and the 1st.

Use the five questions below or create your own. The answers are enclosed in parentheses.

Who was the first African American woman pilot?
(Bessie Coleman, 1893–1926. A top-flight barnstormer in the 1920s, Coleman performed at carnivals and county fairs throughout the U.S., taking the opportunity whenever possible to encourage other African Americans to learn to fly.)

Who was the first African American man recognized nationally as a creative writer?
(Paul Laurence Dunbar, 1872–1906. Dunbar's work, *Complete Poems*, has remained so popular since its publication in 1913 that it has never gone out of print.)

Who was the first African American woman elected to the U.S. Congress?
(Shirley Chisholm, 1924–   . Chisholm served in the House of Representatives from 1966–1982, representing the interests of her urban New York neighborhood, and earning a reputation as an outspoken advocate for women and minorities.)

Which African American man was the first settler and founder of Chicago?
(Jean Baptiste Point duSable, 1745–1818. Point du Sable founded a trading settlement at the site of present day Chicago in 1779.)

Which African American woman was the first to win the Pulitzer Prize?
(Gwendolyn Brooks, 1917–   . Brooks won the Pulitzer Prize for Poetry in 1950 for *Annie Allen,* and continues today to write and to lecture throughout the country.)

Cut 1"-wide strips of green, red, yellow and blue craft paper for the border, using the cutting board. Draw patterns on the border strips with the large black marker. Cut the design strips into different lengths. Then arrange and glue these strips together to form longer strips. Let dry.

Staple light blue craft paper to the board for the background. Pin the border strips, the stars, the letters and the 1st as shown in the illustration. Make sure the question and answer stars match. Staple the proper answer star underneath the correct question star. Staple just the top part of the question star so that it can be easily flipped up to see the answer. Staple the border to the board. Use red bookends to hold the majority of the books. If this display is used in February, then enlarge the sign "February is Black History Month" on red paper using the copier and place it on a bookend near the board.

Books

Display books on African Americans and their achievements.

Supplies

light blue art craft paper for background	scissors
yellow craft paper for stars	red bookends
black craft paper for letters	opaque projector
red craft paper for 1st	stapler
red copier paper for bookmark and sign	pencil / eraser
green, red, yellow and blue craft paper for border	pins
large and medium point black markers	glue
cutting board	copier with enlargement feature

Letter Patterns

AFRICAN AMERICAN FIRSTS

Patterns

February is
Black History
Month

Bookmark

MANY STORIES TO SHARE

When I was about nine years old, my aunt gave me a delicate looking pine needle basket made by the Coushatta Tribe. Gathering a ton of pine needles, I spent hours trying to weave baskets. I was unsuccessful… but, I sure admired the crafters who made the baskets. Louisiana has one of the oldest prehistoric Native American sites–Poverty Point–which is close to the Arkansas border.

Construction

Cut off the bottoms and slice open several large paper bags. Glue the bags together to make enough paper for the totem pole. Let dry. Enlarge the following using the opaque projector: the totem pole on the glued-together paper bags; the mound on the brown craft paper; the pot and the feathers on the white craft paper; the letters, the corn cobs, and the shield animal on the yellow craft paper; the shield on the red craft paper. Draw all in pencil first. Cut 1"-wide strips of black craft paper with the cutting board for the border. Cut out the mound from the brown craft paper.

Draw the designs on the pot and the lines on the feathers, and outline them using a black marker. Color the ends of the feathers with a black colored pencil. Color the pot's flower designs with brown and yellow colored pencils. Cut the pot and the feathers out leaving the black outline.

Outline and draw the details on the corncobs, the letters, the shucks, the shield and the shield animal using a black marker. Color the corncobs' kernels with red, orange and dark brown pencil colors. Cut out all the pieces leaving the black outline. Glue the feathers and the animal to the shield. Glue the corncobs to the shucks.

Draw the designs on the totem pole using a black marker. Color around the mouths, the wing designs and the fish's mouth with red. Color the fish's body and around the totem's eyes a light blue. Cut around the totem pole leaving the black outline.

Enlarge the sign "Celebrate American Indian Heritage Month" on white copier paper using the copier. Next, cut a piece of red art paper about a half inch larger around the edges than the sign. Then glue the sign to the red paper.

Cut light blue craft paper to size of the board and staple it to the board. Pin the mound, then the pot, the totem pole, the letters, the corn cobs, the caption and the shield as shown in the illustration. Staple the border to the board. Use red bookends to hold the majority of the books. If this display is used in November, place the sign "Celebrate American Indian Heritage Month" on a bookend near the board.

Books

Display books on American Indian culture including crafts, foods, shelters, and folk tales.

Supplies

light blue art craft paper for background	stapler
white art craft paper for pot and feathers	pins
large paper bags for totem pole	pencil
yellow art craft paper for letters	opaque projector
red copier paper for bookmark	copier with enlargement feature
manila folders for corn shucks	red bookends
brown art craft paper for mounds	cutting board
black craft paper for border	glue
yellow and red art craft paper for shield, corn, and sign	colored pencils
	black medium point marker
scissors	white copier paper for sign

Letter Patterns

MANY STORIES TO SHARE

Sign

Celebrate American Indian Heritage Month

Patterns

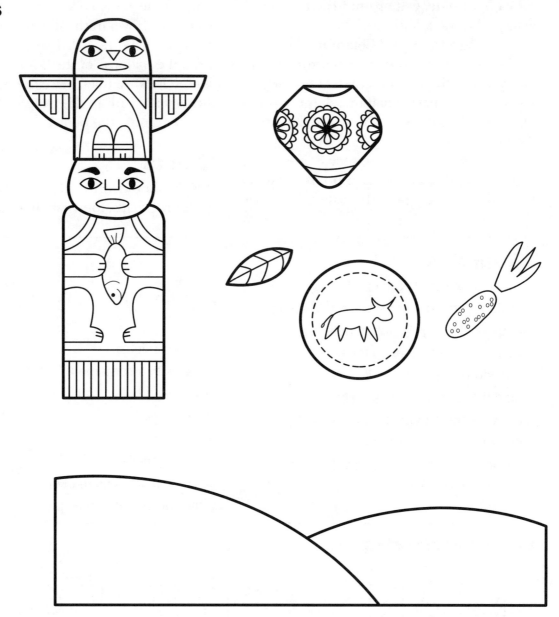

Bookmark

Duplicate bookmark on red copier paper.

Many Stories to Share

Celebrate American Indian Hertiage Month

ONE WORLD, MANY CULTURES

Our world is indeed made up of many cultures; each interesting to learn about and unique in its own way. Our city, Lafayette, has a wonderful multicultural celebration each April. Festival Internationale is a great place for kids and adults to investigate the arts, crafts and cuisine of French-speaking countries. Make sure your exhibit includes cultural groups unique to your area!

Construction

Enlarge the rays and the sun on the white craft paper using the opaque projector. Use these as patterns to trace and cut the the sun out of red foil and the rays out of blue, purple, red, orange and yellow crepe paper. Cut 1"-wide strips of black craft paper with the cutting board for the border.

Cut the green craft paper to the size of the bulletin board. Lay the green craft paper on a flat surface. Place the sun in the upper left-hand corner and the rays radiating from the sun left to right in this order on the green background paper: yellow, orange, red, purple and blue. Glue down all pieces and let dry. Trim the sun and the rays edges if needed. Draw small circles on the sun and short wiggly lines on the rays with the black marker.

Enlarge the letters "One World, Many Cultures" in white craft paper on the copier. Cut out the letters, leaving the black outline, and glue to the background. Look at the illustration for placement. Let dry.

Next, staple the finished background paper to the board. Pin then staple the strips of black craft paper for the border. Yellow bookends can be used to display the books.

NOTE: This board was designed to be used on a square board. It will have to be adjusted to fit different-sized boards. To adjust, simply extend the rays to fit the board's area.

Books

Display books on different countries and cultures. Cookbooks from various countries can also be included.

Supplies

green art craft paper for background

white art craft paper for patterns

white copier paper for letters

blue, purple, red, orange and yellow crepe
    paper for rays

red foil for sun

black medium point marker

black craft paper for border

orange copier paper for bookmark

scissors

stapler

pins

pencil

opaque projector

copier

yellow bookends

glue

cutting board

Letter Patterns

ONE WORLD, MANY CULTURES

Patterns

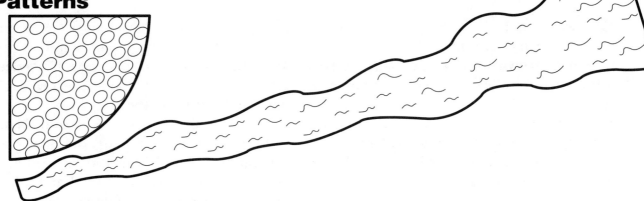

Bookmark

Duplicate bookmark on orange copier paper.

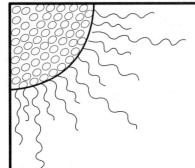

One World,
Many Cultures

In the summer of 1994, we were able to visit Chinatown in San Francisco. What a fabulous place! Such intricate artwork and interesting shops. It was almost like being in China. One day I hope to go back there and spend more time.

Construction

Enlarge all the pattern pieces in pencil using the opaque projector: the lantern on black art paper; the dragon, letters, and kimono details on green art paper; the kimono on magenta art paper; the dragon picture background on yellow art paper; and the dragon picture frame on brown art paper.

Use the black marker to outline the kimono. Draw straight lines on the green kimono details, and random twisting lines on the magenta kimono. Cut out all pieces and glue as shown in illustration.

Outline the dragon and draw woodgrain lines on the brown frames using the black marker. Cut out the dragon, the brown frames and the yellow background. Glue the brown frames and the dragon on the yellow background.

Enlarge the sign on white copier paper using the copier. Next, cut a piece of green art paper to use as backing for the copied sign, allowing ½" border on all sides. Glue the sign to the green paper.

Cut out the letters and the lantern. Then cut out the slits in the black lantern.

Staple the white paper to board for the background. Pin the lantern, kimono, dragon picture, sign, and letters as shown in the illustration. Staple the border to the board. Use black bookends to hold the majority of the books.

Books

Display books on Asian Pacific festivals, foods, crafts, and people.

Supplies

white art craft paper for background

yellow art craft paper for dragon picture

black art craft paper for lantern and border

magenta art craft paper for kimono

green art craft paper for dragon, letters, sign and kimono details

brown art craft paper for dragon picture frame

white copier paper for sign

green copier paper for bookmark

black medium point marker

scissors

black bookends

glue

opaque projector

pins

stapler

paper cutter

pencil

copier with enlargement feature

Letter Patterns

YEARS OF THE DRAGON

Sign

Celebrating Asian Pacific American Heritage Month

Patterns

Bookmark

Print bookmark on green copier paper.

YEARS OF
THE DRAGON